GREATER

LIVING IN THE FULLNESS OF GOD'S PRESENCE

RIVER VALLEY CHURCH

A RIVER VALLEY CHURCH LIFEGROUP SERIES

GREATER

Published by River Valley Church

Editorial Director Don Champion
Senior Editor Lindsay Willis
Editors Jesse Johansen, Clark Strasburg, Clynt Ready
Design and Layout Jessica Nylin

Library of Congress Cataloging-in-Publications Data

ISBN 978-0-9863320-0-5
ISBN 978-0-9863320-1-2 [ebook]

Printed in the United States of America

INTRODUCTION

SESSIONS

APPENDIX

RESOURCES

“I sought to hear the voice of God and climbed the topmost steeple, but God declared: ‘Go down again - I dwell among the people.’”

John Henry Newman

PASTOR ROB & BECCA KETTERLING

HELLO

I am thankful that you've decided to join us for this Greater study. Over these next six weeks, it is my hope and prayer that this small group study will foster unity, align hearts, and inspire us all to pursue a greater presence of God in our everyday lives.

Scripture gives us a key reminder in 1 John 4:4, "The Spirit who lives in you is greater than the spirit who lives in the world." The bottom line is that the presence of God at work in us and through us is more powerful than anything else.

During these six weeks together, we'll examine how God wants us to recognize and live in His Presence in a greater way. We'll explore what it means for us, for those around us, and for the world—because God's presence is everywhere!

We are in for an adventure! Through this study and through the relationships you develop in your group, I'm confident you will be encouraged and challenged. Open up your hearts and minds. Listen to what God is saying to you through the Bible because God is at work in all of us and His presence is Greater!

THE BEST IS YET TO COME!

Rob Ketterling | Lead Pastor

TIPS FOR USING THIS BOOK

STUFF TO HELP YOU HAVE A GREAT GROUP EXPERIENCE:

1. Use this workbook as a guide, not a straight jacket. If your group responds to the lesson in an unexpected but honest way, go with that. If you think of a better question than the next one laid out in the discussion, ask it.

2. If you are leading or co-leading a Greater group, the leader section in the back of this book will give you some valuable tips and encouragement as you lead.

3. Check out the "Session Outline" so you will understand how the sessions and discussions will flow.

4. Enjoy your group! Have fun connecting and growing together.

SESSION OUTLINE

Each session is designed to last anywhere from 60-90 minutes. We structured each meeting with five sections that will help you have a balanced group meeting. A typical Greater session will include:

OPEN UP

This kicks off our group discussion and helps everybody open up on the same page.

TUNE IN

As a group we'll tune in to a weekly video teaching that lays the foundation for the rest of the session.

GO DEEP

If this group were a five-course meal, this would be the entrée. Here we go deep, looking at scripture and sharing personal insights. This is where the magic happens! The group may not use all of the questions and content—think of them as guiding the group along the journey.

PRAY OVER

This is the intersection of this topic and our lives. We encourage the group to share prayer requests and pray for each other's needs during the session and throughout the week.

BUILD ON

This is where we build on the discussion bringing real-life application to the week's content. We take what's in our head and connect it to our heart. We expect a few laughs and a lot of growth as this study comes alive and we discover what it means to live in the fulness of God's presence.

GROUP AGREEMENT

WE WANT OUR EXPERIENCE IN THIS GREATER GROUP TO BE THE BEST IT CAN BE, SO TOGETHER WE AGREE TO THE FOLLOWING:

- We commit to our group to show up at the appointed meeting times, to be on time and end on time. When we cannot attend, we will contact the leaderto let him/her know.
- We will come ready to fully participate in our group.
- We will be sensitive to not dominate group discussions and commit to actively listen when others are talking.
- We will study and discuss scripture in a way that builds up others and brings application to our own lives. We will refuse to judge another person.
- We commit to foster community and candor by maintaining confidentiality. What is said in the group stays in the group, unless permission to share has been given by those involved. [Note: If it is determined that a person is in danger of hurting themselves or someone else, an appropriate Pastor must be notified to help.]
- We will avoid offensive statements and jokes and instead look for opportunities to speak life-giving encouragement to one another.
- We commit to resolve any conflict with someone by working it out directly with that person according to Matthew 18.

SESSION ONE

INTRODUCTION WEEK

Welcome to week one of Greater! In this week, we begin by setting the framework for Greater, as well as develop the environment in which your Greater group will flourish.

Over the next six weeks, God is going to do incredible things in your Greater group. You will experience a great deal of growth individually and collectively. The connections and relationships you develop with your group will be vital to a successful experience during Greater. Take this week to focus on getting to know one another as well as establish the rhythm of your Greater group.

OPEN UP

TAKE THIS TIME FOR GROUP INTRODUCTIONS. MAKE SURE ALL MEMBERS HAVE A CHANCE TO GET TO KNOW ONE ANOTHER!

Have everyone in the group share their name and answer three of the following questions:

- Where did you grow up?
- How long have you been attending our church?
- Did you go school? If so, what for?
- What is your favorite vacation you have ever taken?
- What is one thing you are looking forward to next month?
- If you had to eat one meal every day what would it be?
- What is your favorite book?
- Where is your favorite place to be? Describe it.

Now that you are acquainted, take time to share your hopes and feelings for this Greater study:

- What led you to join a Greater group?
- What is one question you've always had regarding the presence of God?
- What is a topic regarding the presence of God you are eager to discuss and learn about?
- What is something you hope to be different in your own life at the end of this Greater series?

Take some time and walk through the Group Agreement together. If there are any questions about any of these points, feel free to discuss them as a group.

PRAY OVER

LET'S CLOSE IN PRAYER TOGETHER. HERE ARE A COUPLE PRAYER POINTS THIS WEEK. FEEL FREE TO ADD YOUR OWN AS A GROUP.

- Pray we recognize God in the midst of all of our meetings.
- Pray every conversation would be filled with encouragement and truth.
- Pray God would meet us in a new way during the next six weeks.
- Pray God would show us people who may not be in a group that need to be in one.
- Pray for opportunities to invite others to our group.
- ....
- ....
- ....

“We need never shout across the spaces to an absent God. He is nearer than our own soul, closer than our most secret thoughts.”

A.W. Tozer

SESSION TWO

GREATER PRESENCE OF GOD

Welcome to week two of Greater! Today our study will focus on how to recognize the presence of God. Ultimately, there is no place where God is not. Therefore, we must choose daily to tune in to God's presence, which we now have access to through the saving work of Jesus Christ. We will discuss how we best do that, knowing that as we become more aware of His presence in our lives and our world, we draw closer to God.

OPEN UP

WE BEGIN EACH SESSION WITH A QUESTION OR BRIEF ACTIVITY DESIGNED TO HELP US START ON THE SAME PAGE. TAKE TIME TO RECAP LAST WEEK, STARTING WITH INTRODUCTIONS TO HELP EVERYONE GET TO KNOW ONE ANOTHER.

Welcome to week two of Greater. Tonight we will be discussing an age-old question, "Where is God?" Let's get the ball rolling with a quick "where" question of our own:

> WHERE'S YOUR FAVORITE PLACE TO GO WHEN YOU NEED SOME TIME TO RECHARGE?

TUNE IN

Use the space below for notes, questions, or comments you want to bring to the discussion later.

"I HAVE SOMETIMES WONDERED IF THE GREATEST DESIRE OF MAN IS TO BE KNOWN AND LOVED ANYWAY."
Donald Miller

GO DEEP

IT'S TIME TO TALK AND EXPLORE TOGETHER. YOU CAN JOIN THE CONVERSATION BY SHARING YOUR THOUGHTS AND PERSONAL INSIGHTS.

Some questions to discuss:

- Share a story of a time when you experienced God.
- How can we tune into the presence of God?

---

[13] Nothing in all creation is hidden from God. Everything is naked and exposed before his eyes, and he is the one to whom we are accountable. [14] So then, since we have a great High Priest who has entered heaven, Jesus the Son of God, let us hold firmly to what we believe. [15] This High Priest of ours understands our weaknesses, for he faced all of the same testings we do, yet he did not sin. [16] So let us come boldly to the throne of our gracious God. There we will receive his mercy, and we will find grace to help us when we need it most.

Hebrews 4:13-16 (NLT)

In ancient Israel, the high priest functioned as a mediator between God and His people. The high priest was the only person able to enter into the most holy place of the Jewish Temple [a place where the presence of God literally resided]. The priest went in to the presence of God on behalf of the people. So when the author of Hebrews calls Jesus our great high priest, he wants us to understand Jesus as our mediator. Jesus ushers us into the presence of God in a way no high priest was ever able to do before. Through our faith in Christ, we can come boldly to the throne of our gracious God.

Some questions to discuss:

- What is your initial reaction when you hear that nothing is hidden from God?
- Jesus is our High Priest and He understands our weaknesses? What implications does that have for you?
- Who are you accountable to in your job, family, or personal life? How is being accountable to God the same or different?

Our God is everywhere. There is no place where He is not. He is not just here or there. He is everywhere. And the amazing thing about our God is that He desires to know us. He provided a way for us to be in constant, unbroken relationship with Him. This God who is so big and so present desires to be with you. That is the greatness of our God. Nothing is too big for Him...and nothing is too small.

"I USED TO THINK GOD WOULDN'T TALK TO ME, BUT NOW I KNOW I AM JUST SELECTIVE WITH WHAT I CHOOSE TO HEAR."
Bob Goff

Think back to participating in your first sporting event, or recital or play. Remember trying to look for that one person in the audience who would bring you comfort and joy [parents, grandparents, siblings]? Once you saw that person, and knew that he/she was there—everything changed. Your nerves eased and you smiled. That's the reaction we have when we become aware of our ever-present God.

---

1 *God is our refuge and strength, always ready to help in times of trouble.*

Psalm 46:1 (NLT)

Have you ever had trouble? Have you ever received help in a troublesome/bad situation? Could it be that God was your help in that trouble? Could it be that He gave you strength to endure and get through it?

Have you ever asked the question, "Where is God?" How would you answer that question now?

PRAY OVER

LET'S CLOSE IN PRAYER TOGETHER. HERE ARE A COUPLE PRAYER POINTS THIS WEEK. FEEL FREE TO ADD YOUR OWN AS A GROUP.

- No matter where we find ourselves, God is with us.
- We now have acess to the grace-filled presence of God, wherever we are, through Jesus our great High Priest.
- ....
- ....
- ....

BUILD ON

HERE ARE SOME QUICK WINS TO TAKE AWAY FROM THIS WEEK.

A verse to memorize:

8 I know the Lord is always with me. I will not be shaken, for he is right beside me.

Psalm 16:8 (NLT)

An action to take:

Make it your aim, as David did, to recognize that the Lord is always with you. This week, make note of how God demonstrates His presence in your day-to-day life. Celebrate His presence. For He truly is right beside you! Be ready to share what you learned in taking this action step by discussing it next session.

“We may ignore, but we can nowhere evade, the presence of God. The world is crowded with Him. He walks everywhere incognito. And the Incognito is not always easy to penetrate. The real labor is to remember to attend. In fact to come awake. Still more to remain awake.”

C.S. Lewis

SESSION THREE

GREATER PRESENCE OF GOD IN ME

Welcome to week three of Greater! This session looks at experiencing a greater presence of God in our lives. When we step out of the way, there is more room for God. He can then do a greater work in and through our lives. This is really a conversation about space. Are we creating space in our lives so that God can be God? So His presence can be greater?

OPEN UP

WE BEGIN EACH SESSION WITH A QUESTION OR BRIEF ACTIVITY DESIGNED TO HELP US START ON THE SAME PAGE. TAKE TIME TO RECAP LAST WEEK, STARTING WITH INTRODUCTIONS TO HELP EVERYONE GET TO KNOW ONE ANOTHER.

Let's start with a quick icebreaker:

> IF YOU COULD EAT DINNER WITH ANYONE FROM HISTORY [OTHER THAN JESUS] WHO WOULD IT BE? WHAT WOULD YOU TALK ABOUT? WHAT QUESTIONS WOULD YOU ASK?

TUNE IN

Use the space below for notes, questions, or comments you want to bring to the discussion later.

"YOU CAN NEVER GO WHERE GOD IS NOT."
Max Lucado

GO DEEP

IT'S TIME TO TALK AND EXPLORE TOGETHER. JOIN THE CONVERSATION BY SHARING YOUR THOUGHTS AND PERSONAL INSIGHTS.

Some questions to discuss:

- Why do we find it so hard to make room for God in our every day life?
- How can we make more room for God?

---

22 Then Jesus and his disciples left Jerusalem and went into
the Judean countryside. Jesus spent some time with them
there, baptizing people. 23 At this time John the Baptist was
baptizing at Aenon, near Salim, because there was plenty of
water there; and people kept coming to him for baptism. 24
[This was before John was thrown into prison.] 25 A debate
broke out between John's disciples and a certain Jew over
ceremonial cleansing. 26 So John's disciples came to him and
said, "Rabbi, the man you met on the other side of the Jordan
River, the one you identified as the Messiah, is also baptizing
people. And everybody is going to him instead of coming to us."
27 John replied, "No one can receive anything unless God gives
it from heaven. 28 You yourselves know how plainly I told you, 'I
am not the Messiah. I am only here to prepare the way for him.'
29 It is the bridegroom who marries the bride, and the best man
is simply glad to stand with him and hear his vows. Therefore,
I am filled with joy at his success. 30 He must become greater
and greater, and I must become less and less.

John 3:22-30 (NLT)

In this story, we find John the Baptist doing what he was most known for: baptizing. People came from all around to be baptized by him. "The fact people" were now going to Jesus to be baptized created genuine concern among the disciples of John .The disciples are promptly reminded that the success and glory of John the Baptist was not the end goal. His goal was to prepare the way for Jesus.

Some questions to discuss:

- Put yourself in the shoes of one of John the Baptist's disciples. How might you have reacted in this situation?
- Why do you think John chose the illustration of a groom and his best man to demonstrate his relationship to Jesus? How might this illustration demonstrate our own relationship with Jesus?
- How can you prepare the way for Jesus in your life?

Are we laying ourselves down in a greater way so that God can rise up in a greater way? Every gift, every talent, every blessing we have comes from God. It can be so easy to lean on what we already have, taking credit for what God has freely given. Like the disciples of John the Baptist, we are prone to worry about our own place in the world, losing sight of God's mission.

Our own idea of success must take a back seat to God's idea of success. His Spirit propels us forward, giving a greater recognition of God's presence in us. Once we create space for God to be greater in our life, we can't help but be changed by His presence.

Is the way that we live creating space for more of God's presence in our daily lives?

PRAY OVER

LET'S CLOSE IN PRAYER TOGETHER. HERE ARE A COUPLE PRAYER POINTS THIS WEEK. FEEL FREE TO ADD YOUR OWN AS A GROUP.

- God is greater in our lives when we live in obedience to His will.
- There is nothing greater than the will of God for our lives.
- ....
- ....
- ....

BUILD ON

HERE ARE SOME QUICK WINS TO TAKE AWAY FROM THIS WEEK.

A verse to memorize:

[8] Remain in me, and I will remain in you. For a branch cannot produce fruit if it is severed from the vine, and you cannot be fruitful unless you remain in me.

John 15:4 (NLT)

An action to take:

Model yourself after John the Baptist, having selfless joy in the work of Jesus Christ. Make a conscious effort to lift up Jesus in your life and celebrate the nearness of His presence. Be ready to share what you learned in taking this action step by discussing it next session.

"Your restless heart will only find rest when it rests in the person, presence and promises of Jesus."

Paul Tripp

SESSION FOUR

GREATER PRESENCE OF GOD IN US

Welcome to week four of Greater! This week we will discuss what it means to live a life of worship. For many of us, the word "worship" is usually connected to a time of singing and praising God together. But the word "worship" actually means so much more. Worship ultimately exposes the posture of our hearts, which we live out with our words and deeds. Worship is not just a moment, worship is a lifestyle.

OPEN UP

WE BEGIN EACH SESSION WITH A QUESTION OR BRIEF ACTIVITY DESIGNED TO HELP US START ON THE SAME PAGE. TAKE TIME TO RECAP LAST WEEK, STARTING WITH INTRODUCTIONS TO HELP EVERYONE GET TO KNOW ONE ANOTHER.

This week we discuss what it means to worship God with all we have. First, take a moment to recap from last week.

WHAT WAS ONE WAY YOU CREATED SPACE FOR GOD TO BE GREATER BY YOU BECOMING LESS? HOW DID YOU MAKE CHRIST GREATER IN YOUR LIFE?

TUNE IN

Use the space below for notes, questions, or comments you want to bring to the discussion later.

"ALL THAT WE CALL HUMAN HISTORY [MONEY, POVERTY, AMBITION, WAR, PROSTITUTION, CLASSES, EMPIRES, SLAVERY] IS THE LONG, TERRIBLE STORY OF MAN TRYING TO FIND SOMETHING OTHER THAN GOD WHICH WILL MAKE HIM HAPPY."
C.S. Lewis

GO DEEP

IT'S TIME TO TALK AND EXPLORE TOGETHER. JOIN THE CONVERSATION BY SHARING YOUR THOUGHTS AND PERSONAL INSIGHTS.

Some questions to discuss:

- What value do you find in the worship time in church?
- How does the idea of worshipping God as you move through your life change your perspective on worship?

> *[14]For this world is not our permanent home; we are looking forward to a home yet to come. [15] Therefore, let us offer through Jesus a continual sacrifice of praise to God, proclaiming our allegiance to his name. [16] And don't forget to do good and to share with those in need. These are the sacrifices that please God.*

Hebrews 13:14-16 (NLT)

The author of Hebrews makes it clear that worship is both singing praises with our lips as well as being a world-changer with our hands. In other words, we sell ourselves short of the fullness of worship when we limit its practice to something we just do on the weekends. God calls us to continually offer praise to Him both in our words and in our deeds. Worship is not a moment; it is a lifestyle.

Some questions to discuss:

- What would it look like to live a life of worship?
- What do you think it means to proclaim our allegiance to God?
- Why is the word sacrifice used so often in these verses [Romans 12:2 & Hebrews 14: 16], and what might that tell us about worship?

Sacrifice challenges our perspective on worship. Sacrifice is best described as giving up something valued for the sake of something more important or worthy. Sacrifice exposes our priorities and values.

For the ancient Israelites, sacrifice was a normal part of their worship. Oftentimes, worshippers would bring animals to the Temple to be sacrificed. These animals would be offered to God as a symbol of surrender and mercy. By doing this, the Israelites communicated that obeying God's commands was of greater value than their possessions. In a society dominated by agriculture, this said a lot. Israel's priority was, first and foremost God.

> *"NO MATTER HOW MANY GOOD DEEDS WE PERFORM, THEY AREN'T THE TICKET TO EARNING GOD'S FAVOR. GOD GRACES US IN SPITE OF WHAT WE DO IN THIS LIFE, NOT BECAUSE OF IT."*
> **Bill Courtney**

As we worship God with our lives, what are we willing to give up for Him? Jesus sacrificed His life on our behalf. This is why He is worthy of honor and praise and glory. He is our ultimate example of selflessness, humility, and love. He is our ultimate example of a life of worship to God.

- What is one area of your life that you should invite God into as an act of worship?

---

[2] Live a life filled with love, following the example of Christ. He loved us and offered himself as a sacrifice for us, a pleasing aroma to God.

EPHESIANS 5:2 (NLT)

Our worship—the living sacrifice we offer to God—is a pleasing aroma to Him. When we worship God with everything by offering all to Him, we bring pleasure to Him.

How will our lives look different when we live a life of worship—sacrificed, surrendered and yielded to Him?

PRAY OVER

LET'S CLOSE IN PRAYER TOGETHER. HERE ARE A COUPLE PRAYER POINTS THIS WEEK. FEEL FREE TO ADD YOUR OWN AS A GROUP.

- We want to connect more deeply with God in worship at church.
- We want to live a life of worship everday of the week.
- We want God to reveal areas of our life in which we have yet to sacrifice and fully surrender to Him.
- ....
- ....
- ....

BUILD ON

HERE ARE SOME QUICK WINS TO TAKE AWAY FROM THIS WEEK.

A verse to memorize:

[1] Take your everyday, ordinary life-your sleeping, eating, going-to-work, and walking-around life-and place it before God as an offering.

Romans 12:1 (THE MESSAGE)

An action to take:

Look for opportunities this week to live out worship to God in your everyday life. Be ready to share what you learned in taking this action step by discussing it at our next Greater Group.

"It's not the art, it's the heart. What God reads during our worship is the inner attitude. Worship is spiritual; it's organic; it's relational."

LaMar Boschman

SESSION FIVE

GREATER PRESENCE OF GOD THROUGH US

Welcome to week five of Greater! This week is all about the presence of God working through us to impact those around us. God is writing an amazing story in the world. He brings new life to His people and reconciles all things back to Himself. As believers, we are not merely products but partakers in this great mission. God is inviting us to work with Him in setting the world to right.

OPEN UP

WE BEGIN EACH SESSION WITH A QUESTION OR BRIEF ACTIVITY DESIGNED TO HELP US START ON THE SAME PAGE. TAKE TIME TO RECAP LAST WEEK, STARTING WITH INTRODUCTIONS TO HELP EVERYONE GET TO KNOW ONE ANOTHER.

We will discuss how the Presence of God works through us, reverberating through others near and far in the greater world. As we dive in, take a moment to share any stories about last week's action to take.

WHAT WAS ONE WAY YOU WORSHIPPED GOD WITH YOUR EVERY DAY LIFE?

TUNE IN

Use the space below for notes, questions or comments you want to bring to the discussion later.

"THE SON OF GOD BECAME A MAN TO ENABLE MEN TO BECOME SONS OF GOD."
C.S. Lewis

GO DEEP

IT'S TIME TO TALK AND EXPLORE TOGETHER. JOIN THE CONVERSATION BY SHARING YOUR THOUGHTS AND PERSONAL INSIGHTS.

Some questions to discuss:

- Identify a gift that God has given you. What role do these gifts play in carrying the presence of God wherever we go?

---

[1] If I could speak all the languages of earth and of angels, but didn't love others, I would only be a noisy gong or a clanging cymbal. [2] If I had the gift of phophecy, and if I understood all of God's secret plans and possessed all knowledge, and if I had such faith I could move mountains, but didn't love others, I would be nothing. [3] If I gave everything I have to the poor and even sacrifice my body, I could boast about it; but if I didn't love others, I would have gained nothing.

1 Corinthians 13:1-3 (NLT)

- What impact do gifts have in a collective, community setting?

---

[24] So God has put the body together such that extra honor and care are given to those parts that have less dignity. [25] This makes for harmony among the members, so that all the members care for each other. [26] If one part suffers, all the parts suffer with it, and if one part is honored, all the parts are glad. [27] All of you together are Christ's body, and each of you is a part of it.

1 Corinthians 12:24-27 (NLT)

Share a story of a time when a seemingly simple gift had a big impact on the life of you or someone else.

These two passages highlight important aspects about spiritual gifts. First, spiritual gifts are not intended to operate in isolation but within the body of Christ to accomplish God's will in the world. Our gifts reach their fullest potential when they bring others into cooperation.

Secondly, spiritual gifts cannot be effective if they are without love. The entire existence of spiritual gifts in the first place is to bring the love of God into the world. In the original text of this passage, the word for "spiritual gifts" (charismata) stems from the Greek word charis, meaning "grace." Any spiritual gift, at it's simplest, is nothing more than a divine expression of grace, a gift wrapped in love. When we love others, God can work through us so that others can experience His love. Our acts of love, no matter how big or small, create opportunities for people to experience God's love for them.

"WE OUGHT NOT BE WEARY OF DOING LITTLE THINGS FOR THE LOVE OF GOD, WHO REGARDS NOT THE GREATNESS OF THE WORK, BUT THE LOVE WITH WHICH IT IS PERFORMED."
Brother Lawrence

Some questions to discuss:

- How might the presence of God in us help bring reconciliation to the world?
- What are some practical ways we can love one another, so that we create opportunities for people around us to experience God's presence?

PRAY OVER

LET'S CLOSE IN PRAYER TOGETHER. HERE ARE A COUPLE PRAYER POINTS THIS WEEK. FEEL FREE TO ADD YOUR OWN AS A GROUP.

- God helps us see opportunitiies to love others, even in small ways.
- God uses our acts of love so that other people may experience His presence, some for the first time.
- ....
- ....

BUILD ON

HERE ARE SOME QUICK WINS TO TAKE AWAY FROM THIS WEEK.

A verse to memorize:

17 This means that anyone who belongs to Christ has become a new person. The old life, is gone, and the new life has begun!

2 Corinthians 5:17 [NLT]

An action to take:

Take an opportunity to show love to someone who might be in need. Maybe someone you know is in a tough situation or could use a friend. Ask God to use you to demonstrate His love for them. Watch as God uses you to love others in a way that only He could!

> "Here is the original design. The Breathe of Life comes to us, indwells and empowers us, and flows through us. We represent [think "re-present"] God on Earth, and He accomplishes His plans through us."

Bob Hamp

SESSION SIX

GREATER CELEBRATION

CELEBRATION

It's time to celebrate! There is no doubt that God has done amazing things in you and in your Greater group. That is cause for a celebration. How you celebrate is up to you. Go out to a restaurant together; enjoy appetizers, a meal or a dessert [or all three] at someone's home; head out to a favorite coffee shop or spot around town. No matter how you decide to celebrate just remember to relax with one another, reflect and, share all the winning moments from the past six weeks.

Here are a few things we'd love for your group to talk about:

- Share stories about how you saw God work through Greater.
- How has God changed your perspective on His presence?
- How is your life different because of this Greater group?
- What prayers were answered during this series?
- How has God's presence shown you the best is yet to come?
- What two or three areas do you want to see God change in you during the rest of the year?

"It's when people do not allow God to show up through them...that the world collapses on it-self."

Donald Miller

WHAT'S NEXT?

We do not want Greater to be just a spike in your spiritual life. We want it to be the beginning of a new adventure in becoming a more devoted follower of Jesus Christ. At River Valley, there are many options and avenues for you to continue on this journey! We know it can be a little daunting to identify what the best next step for you will be. To help you with that, we have created the GROW Assessment.

The GROW Assessment takes about 12-15 minutes to complete. It simply creates a catalog of your spiritual strengths and areas of potential growth. It will also provide you with a personalized list of Lifegroups and resources that are excellent next steps for you on your journey to becoming a more devoted Christ follower.

You can find the GROW Assessment at: **grow.rivervalley.org**

APPENDIX

FAQ

WHAT DO WE DO ON THE FIRST NIGHT OF GROUP?
Start off with relationship. Your Greater group might need to spend some time getting to know one another. Plan extra time for introductions and create a relaxed social atmosphere up front for people to get to know one another. Remember we want you to be connected with one another, so a little fun and socializing is a great way to start.

WHERE DO I FIND NEW MEMBERS FOR MY GROUP?
We always say that the best way to find members for your group is to look for people already in your proximity. Brainstorm a list of people you could invite from your work, your neighborhood, your family, your child's school, your gym and so on.

HOW LONG WILL THIS GROUP MEET?
It's totally up to the group once you come to the end of this six-week study. During the Greater series your group will meet weekly and after those six weeks it's our hope that your group will continue to meet either weekly or every other week, we encourage both.

At the end of this study, each group member may decide if he or she wants to continue on for another study. Some groups launch relationships for years to come, and other are stepping-stones into another group experience. Either way, enjoy the journey.

WHAT IF THIS GROUP IS NOT WORKING FOR US?
Don't worry, you are not alone! This can often be the result of geographical distance, life-stage difference, personality conflict, level of spiritual maturity or a number of other things. Take a deep breath. You don't always buy the first car you look at or marry the first person you date, and the same goes with your group. Don't bail out before the six weeks are up - God might be looking to teach you something. Be careful not to quickly judge people or run from conflict--remember we're all a work in progress. Seek God in the process and extend grace to one another.

WHO IS THE LEADER?
There is a designated or official leader for each group. That person gets the final call. That said, we have found that in the healthiest groups, leaders share responsibility. This ensures that all members grow, giving their unique contribution and developing their gifts. Ultimately, we recognize God's leadership in the group and give him thanks for every breakthrough the group sees.

HOW DO WE HANDLE CHILDCARE NEEDS IN OUR GROUP?
With careful deliberation, knowing this can be a sensitive issue. We suggest empowering the group to openly brainstorm solutions - this is a good discussion to start when you meet. You may try one option that works for a while and then adjust it over time. Our favorite approach is for adults to meet in the living room or dining room, sharing the cost of a babysitter (or two) who can be with the kids in a different part of the house. In this way parents don't have to be away from their children all evening when their children are too young to be left at home. A second option is to use one home for the kids and a second home (close by or a phone call away) for the adults. A third idea is to rotate the responsibility of providing a lesson or care for the children between group members in another home or room of the house. Finally, a common idea is to decide that you need to have a night to invest in your spiritual lives individually or as a couple, and to make your own arrangements for childcare. No matter what decision the group makes, the best approach is to dialogue openly about the plan.

PRAYER REQUESTS & PRAISE REPORTS

WEEK ONE:

WEEK TWO:

WEEK THREE:

-
-
-
-
-
-
-
-
-
-
-
-
-
-
-

WEEK FOUR:

WEEK FIVE:

KEY VERSES

WEEK 1
Genesis 1:2 [NLT], "The earth was formless and empty, and darkness covered the deep waters. And the Spirit of God was hovering over the surface of the waters."

WEEK 2
Psalm 16:8 [NLT], "I know the LORD is always with me. I will not be shaken, for he is right beside me."

WEEK 3
John 3:30 [NLT], "He must become greater and greater, and I must become less and less."

WEEK 4
Romans 12:1 [The Message], "Take your everyday, ordinary life - your sleeping, eating, going-to-work, and walking-around life - and place it before God as an offering."

WEEK 5
2 Corinthians 5:17 [NLT], "This means that anyone who belongs to Christ has become a new person. The old life is gone, and the new life has begun!"

WEEK 6
Ephesians 3:20 [NLT], "Now all glory to God, who is able, through his mighty power at work within us, to accomplish infinitely more than we might ask or think."

"He must become GREATER and GREATER, and I must become less and less."

John 3:30

LEADER RESOURCES

LEADING A GREAT GROUP 101

THINK FACILITATOR

Leading a group is all about being a good facilitator. You don't have to have all the answers but you do have to give every person an opportunity to contribute and feel valued. That will happen most effectively when you ask great questions and tie together the responses of those around you. Grow as a facilitator and watch your group thrive.

PREPARE AND PRAY

Master the art of working like it depends on you and praying like it depends on God. Put your best foot forward every week. Come prepared to lead with excellence. Be prepared spiritually. But don't think it is all about you. Stay grounded in prayer for each person in your group.

YOU'RE NOT ALONE

Leading a group may seem like an intimidating thing, especially if this is your first time. We all have friends, leaders, and pastors to help you prepare and lead your group well. Keep in mind that you also have the Holy Spirit guiding you every step of the way. Lean on Him as you prepare and facilitate your group experience.

LEAD THE WAY IN HOSPITALITY

Lead by example here. Take every opportunity to shower your group participants with hospitality. Make sure you welcome and connect with each participant during the meetings. In addition, have some snacks or drinks available when your group arrives. (Feel free to ask others in the group to help you make this happen from week to week). Hospitality doesn't have to cost a lot of money. Have an attitude of joy and love because you are a host as well as a leader.

GO SMALLER

Helping others find community through meeting together is a great win for your Greater group. Even in the smaller setting of a group, seize the opportunity to find even smaller groups within your small group. These smaller groups can more effectively pray for one another and hold each other accountable.

EMBRACE THE SILENCE

Silence is going to happen. Questions, especially at first, will usually be met by silence rather than an outpouring of responses, so be prepared for that. It's okay to have silence in a group setting. Don't try to break the silence by giving your response. Silence can be a healthy part of the group dynamic. Try to leverage it to create vibrant discussion.

RAISE UP SOMEONE ELSE

Every group has an opportunity to raise up and equip a leader for the Kingdom of God. Each one of us was created with an ability to serve and influence others, which are two indispensable qualities of great leaders. Have other group members lead the discussion of a question. Engage potential leaders in conversation to gauge their interest in leading another group. You always have an emerging leader in your midst.

BE YOU

God created you uniquely because you are destined to leave a unique mark on this world. God has further led you to this moment, where you have a chance to influence those in your Lifegroup. So don't try to be someone you're not. God placed you here for a reason. People want to know the true you. Love who you are and encourage others to do the same.

LOVE THE PEOPLE AROUND YOU

Don't forget that you have been entrusted with God's most precious creation—people. Now don't feel burdened by that because there is no such thing as a perfect leader. God did not call you to lead those in your Lifegroup because you're perfect. He called you to love those around you. Take every chance to love your group members. Pray for them whenever you can.

CELEBRATE THE WINS

What's celebrated is repeated, so celebrate the wins in your group. Celebrate when prayer is answered, when leaders step up, when group members come prepared, when everyone participates. Use celebration as a strategic opportunity to model great group behavior to those around you.